ELITE
SPECIAL
FORCES

Bruce Quarrie

A QUINTET BOOK

ISBN: 1-85348-837-2

This book was designed and produced by
Quintet Publishing Limited

Creative Director: Peter Bridgewater
Art Director: Ian Hunt
Designer: James Lawrence
Jacket Design: Nik Morley

Typeset in Great Britain by
Central Southern Typesetters, Eastbourne

Produced in Australia by Griffin Colour

Published by Selectabook Limited,
Devizes.

Contents

The tradition of elite military forces stretches in an unbroken line from the Praetorian Guard of the Caesars through Napoleon's Imperial Old Guard to Britain's Brigade of Guards and other modern equivalents. Within every army in history there have been one or two units which, because of superior fighting skill, loyalty and discipline, have been considered a 'cut above' the rest. On the battlefield such troops would generally be held in reserve ready either to administer the coup de grâce when the enemy was on the point of defeat, or to act as an intact rallying point for the remainder of the army in case things went wrong. During and since the Second World War, however, a different type of elite force has emerged which recruits from within the existing elite, and it is with these that this book is concerned.

During the First World War, when the fighting on the Western Front bogged down in the stalemate of the trenches, the German army pioneered the use of small raiding parties. These were compact groups of veteran volunteers who, unencumbered with all the infantryman's heavy kit but armed to the teeth instead with close-quarter weapons, would sneak through the barbed wire at night to fall on an unsuspecting stretch of Allied trench, kill everyone in sight and retreat back into no man's land before reserves could be rushed to the spot. It was for the use of such troops that the first sub-machine gun was developed.

These Stosstruppen, or stormtroopers, as they were called, formed the model for the 'kommandos' of Hitler's feared Waffen-SS. Under Otto Skorzeny, their exploits included the daring rescue of Mussolini when he was being held by Italian partisans in a mountain-top hotel, and a lightning raid on Tito's headquarters in Yugoslavia. This only failed because the leader of the communist resistance was not there at the time. They also kidnapped Hungarian Regent Admiral Horthy's son from a fortress in the heart of Budapest to stiffen the Hungarian government's resolve to continue fighting the Russians. Skorzeny's 150th Brigade also took part in the Battle of the Bulge at the end of 1944 when many of its men, dressed in American army uniforms and driving American vehicles, were caught and subsequently shot as spies. Ironically, one of the two principal SS officer training schools in what is now West Germany, Bad Tölz, is today used by the American Rangers!

The German army and air force created their own special forces apart from these Waffen-SS commandos. Italy had pioneered the use of the parachute as a method of dropping troops into battle in the 1920s and the Soviet Union had eagerly adopted the idea. German observers were particularly impressed by a Soviet exercise near Kiev in 1935 in which 2,500 paratroopers dropped to secure an airfield and hold it while reinforcements were flown in. As a direct result, the Germans spurred on their researches into military gliders and formed their first parachute battalion in January 1936. By 1940 there were five battalions, which played a major role in the conquest of Norway in April and France and the Low Countries in May, dropping ahead of the regular ground forces to secure bridges and airfields. They also landed on top of the supposedly impregnable Belgian fortress of Eben Emael, whose garrison was so stunned that a thousand men surrendered with hardly a fight to a mere 85 men, only six German soldiers being killed. German paras subsequently went on to fight in North Africa, Italy and Russia, their most famous achievement being the aerial conquest of Crete in May 1941.

The German army had also realized the importance of special forces to race ahead and seize key objectives in advance of the Panzer divisions in their planned Blitzkrieg ('lightning war'). At the beginning of 1939 the head of the Abwehr (military intelligence), Admiral Wilhelm Canaris, formed a company of predominantly Polish-speaking volunteers who, dressed in Polish uniforms, seized key bridges and rail junctions in Poland on 1 September that year. This tiny unit eventually grew to the size of a regiment, the 'Brandenburg' Regiment, and carried out many similar operations during the invasions of Belgium in 1940 and Russia in 1941. Modelling themselves on Lawrence of Arabia, who was one of the earliest modern exponents of unconventional warfare, in 1942 a small party of Brandenburgers made an epic 2,000-mile trek across the Sahara to escort a pair of German agents into Cairo, and in 1943 the regiment spearheaded the assault on the island of Leros in the Aegean.

Unfortunately for them, the necessities of war eventually saw the cream of the German elite forces frittered away in ordinary infantry actions as the Allies chipped away at the frontiers of the Third Reich.

The Second World War also saw the raising of similar units in the armies of other countries. Immediately after the fall of France in June 1940 a Colonel on the British General Staff, Dudley Clarke, pressed for a reorganization of the earlier Independent Companies which had been created in the spring of the 'Phoney War' for behind-the-lines sabotage operations. No 3 Commando, led by Lieutenant-Colonel John Durnford-Slater, was the result, the name 'commando' deriving from the groups of irregular soldiers who had fought the Boers in South Africa at the turn of the century. What would have been No 1 Commando was formed from the Independent Companies and, five battalions strong, was originally given the rather unfortunate name Special Service (SS) Brigade, although this was abandoned during 1941. Similarly, the original No 2 Commando formed the nucleus of the new British airborne force which Prime Minister Winston Churchill had ordered created on 22 June 1940.

During the course of the war the number of army commando battalions was expanded to 12 (there was also a 13th, superstitiously numbered No 14 Commando, for a brief time), plus a further three in the Middle East (Nos 50, 51 and 52 [ME]). The Royal Marines also formed nine between 1942 and 1944 numbered 40 to 40 (RM), and more than 18,000 army and Marine Commandos took part in the invasion of Normandy in 1944. Nos 10 and 51 Commandos were the most unusual. The first was an inter-allied force of mixed nationalities which even included a number of anti-Nazi German volunteers, serving under false identities in case of capture. The latter was a mixed force of Palestinian Arab and Jewish volunteers with British officers which principally fought in East Africa.

One obvious criterion for any elite force is that its members should all be volunteers because the nature of their tasks demands a very high level of motivation and self-discipline. It was in recognition of these qualities that the wearing of the distinctive green Commando beret was authorized after the Dieppe raid in August 1942.

Meanwhile, what would have been No 2 Commando had mustered at Ringway, near Manchester, in July 1940 and in November was renamed No 11 Special Air Service Battalion. This title was dropped in September 1941 and the unit became 1st Battalion, 1st Parachute Brigade, commanded by Lieutenant-Colonel E E 'Dracula' Down. The 2nd Battalion was originally commanded by Lieutenant-Colonel E W C Flavell and subsequently by an officer whose name has become synonymous with wartime parachute exploits, Major John Frost. The 3rd Battalion was led by Lieutenant-Colonel G W Lathbury.

Then came the formation of the Glider Pilot Regiment in December as a further step towards the creation of the 1st Airborne Division which Churchill had demanded after the loss of Crete had demonstrated what parachute and glider forces could achieve. In August 1942 the para battalions became The Parachute

Regiment and, envious of the Commandos' green beret, they adopted a maroon one as their own trademark. By the time of D-Day there were two complete divisions, the 1st commanded by Major-General Roy Urquhart and the 6th under Major-General Richard Gale. Overall commander of airborne forces was Brigadier F A M 'Boy' Browning.

The commandos and the airborne forces established formidable reputations during the Second World War and their modern successors have continued the tradition, as we shall see. There is no space here to describe their wartime exploits – the Lofoten Islands' raid, Vaagso, St Nazaire (which resulted in the award of five Victoria Crosses), Dieppe, the invasions of French North-West Africa and Sicily, Normandy, Arnhem, Comacchio, etc, not to mention smaller-scale adventures such as Bruneval, when a combined airborne/commando force raided a German radar installation in northern France to bring its secrets back for the 'boffins'. There are many fine books on these operations, several written by the men who actually took part in them.

Going back to 1941, however, we find the 'Special Air Service' (SAS) title revived in North Africa – this time permanently. The early history of what is widely regarded as the ultimate elite military formation of modern times deserves special attention. Nos 7, 8 and 11 Commandos had been sent to Egypt in the spring of that year to help counter the German forces under Erwin Rommel, despatched by Hitler to aid his hapless ally, Mussolini. They were generally known as 'Layforce' after their commander, Major-General Robert Laycock, but were soon split up, No 11 going to Cyprus while No 7 joined 50 and 52 (ME) Commandos on Crete. Most of the men of the latter three units were killed or captured fighting a valiant rearguard action when the German paras landed in May, which just left No 8 in Egypt. One of its junior officers was Lieutenant David Stirling.

Kicking his heels wondering what to do after the fall of Crete, he and three friends decided to try their own hands at parachuting. Unfortunately, Stirling's parachute failed to deploy properly on his first jump and he had to spend several weeks in hospital. While languishing there he evolved the concept of tiny raiding parties of no more than four or five men, which would be far more elusive than a regular Commando company of 50 or so. These could be dropped by parachute or infiltrated by Jeeps or small boats, deep behind enemy lines to carry out reconnaissance or sabotage missions. When he left hospital Stirling managed to persuade General Sir Claude Auchinleck, C-in-C in the Western Desert, of the validly of his ideas, which remain the cornerstone of all special

PREVIOUS PAGE Colonel (now Sir) David Stirling (right) with a section of SAS men in their famous 'Pink Panther' Jeeps in North Africa. ABOVE A corporal of the Long Range Desert Group nurses the twin Lewis machine-guns in his Jeep. Chevrolet trucks were also widely used.

forces to this day. The result was 'L' Detachment, Special Air Service Brigade. There was, in fact, no longer an SAS Battalion, let alone Brigade. The name was a ploy to make Rommel think that a strong British parachute force had arrived in North Africa. The name stuck and soon there were two full SAS regiments, the 1st under Major R B 'Paddy' Mayne (after David Stirling was captured in January 1943), the 2nd by Stirling's brother Bill.

Stirling's SAS shared many exploits with the Long Range Desert Group (formed in December 1940 by Major Ralph Bagnold) and 'Popski's Private Army', the force of Libyan Arab commandos led by Belgian-born expatriate Russian Major Vladimir Peniakoff. Their officers and men freely exchanged ideas and evolved hard-hitting tactics for behind-the-lines operations against German and Italian airfields and fuel dumps. These tactics would be honed and refined over the years in many battles around the world, particularly in the modern fight against terrorism in which the SAS is the acknowledged master. It was in the camaraderie of this environment that the enlisted men of the SAS learned to call their officers by the now cherished title 'boss', which soon puts any Sandhurst superman in his place! The present day Royal Marines' Special Boat Squadron is also part of the early story for it originally evolved from a tiny component of 'Layforce' as part of Stirling's inaugural SAS. The British created dozens of similar small units for longer or shorter periods during the war but only the SAS and SBS have retained their identities and the two – elites within an elite – maintain close links alongside the usual friendly rivalry.

After fighting in the desert and later carrying out many daring penetration missions in Italy, the two SAS regiments were returned to the UK and brigaded together with a Belgian squadron and two Free French parachute battalions to form the 1st Special Air Service Brigade – now a reality rather than a codename. Working closely with SOE – the Strategic Operations Executive – and resistance groups in occupied Europe, they carried out dozens of invaluable reconnaissance and sabotage missions both before and after D-Day, their teams often operating 50 miles and more ahead of the front line in constant dread of detection.

Entering the war later than the UK, the United States was, surprisingly, quicker to begin to develop similar forces. The first plans for a test platoon of paratroopers were approved in April 1940 but it was not until July, following the fall of France, that things really started moving. Even then progress was slow because America still hoped to stay out of another European war. The platoon did not make its first drop from an aircraft until August and establishment of a proper training school at Fort Benning did not occur until the following April. By the time of the Japanese attack on Pearl Harbor there was still only one operational battalion, the 501st. Their jump word of 'Geronimo!' remains part of the US airborne forces' tradition to this day.

The spring of 1942 saw a huge leap forward and the creation of another 26 consecutively numbered battalions, many of whose officers and men visited England to witness British training methods and results and to meet their allied opposite numbers. By August two embryo divisions existed, the battalions having grown to regimental strength. These were the 82nd ('All Americans') commanded initially by Major-General Omar N Bradley and subsequently by Brigadier-General Matthew B Ridgway, and the 101st ('Screaming Eagles') commanded by Lieutenant-Colonel (later Brigadier-General) William C Lee. Their first operation came when a battalion of 503rd Regiment of the 82nd parachuted in to capture an airfield in Tunisia following Operation 'Torch', the Anglo-American invasion of French North-West Africa in November 1942. Elements of both divisions took part in many subsequent operations in Sicily and Italy before being withdrawn to England for D-Day when, alongside the British 6th Airborne Division, they landed on the French coast in advance of the main amphibious assault.

They subsequently took part in the bold attempt to cross the Rhine codenamed 'Market Garden', the 82nd landing to secure bridges at Nijmegen and the 101st at Eindhoven. The American end of the operation was a success but the unfortunate British 1st Airborne which dropped at Arnhem found itself confronted by an entire SS Panzer division and, lacking tanks or other heavy equipment, was unable to secure its objective despite a heroic fight. Withdrawn to rest and recuperate, the two American airborne divisions were the only forces in a position to help when Field Marshal Gerd von Rundstedt's Panzer divisions struck unexpectedly through the Ardennes just before Christmas. The 101st raced to secure the road junction at Bastogne, while the 82nd took the one at St Vith, and between them they slowed the German advance until relieved by General George S Patton Jr's Third Army. It was at Bastogne that General Anthony McAuliffe delivered the famous reply 'Nuts!' when called upon to surrender.

Meanwhile, a third airborne division had been created from the First Airborne Task Force, the 17th, commanded first by Major-General Robert T Frederick and then by Major-General William Miley. The Anglo-American Task Force had been formed in Italy for Operation 'Dragoon', the invasion of southern France in August 1944, after which the British component had returned to Italy but the new 17th remained in France. It was rushed to help in the drive to relieve the 101st at Bastogne and subsequently fought its way into Germany after dropping alongside the British 6th Airborne in March 1945 to secure the Rhine crossings.

Finally, on the other side of the world a single regiment, the 503rd, had sailed to Australia after its battles in Tunisia and formed the nucleus of the 11th Airborne Division which fought the Japanese at Leyte, Luzon, Corregidor ('The Rock') and Okinawa under Major-General Joseph M Swing. After the war all the airborne divisions except the 82nd were disbanded although the 101st was subsequently reactivated as an 'Airmobile' division, equipped with helicopters, for the war in Vietnam.

While the US airborne forces were being built up in 1942, a new type of elite unit was also in the process of being created: the Rangers. Their name has its origins in the force formed in 1756 by Major Robert Rogers as a light, fast-moving unit to fight for the then British colonies against the French and Indians. The 1st Battalion of this now illustrious American formation was raised in June 1942 in Northern Ireland. General George C Marshall, impressed by the exploits of British Commandos and anxious that American troops should get a foretaste of battle before any major operations took place, chose a Major from the staff of the 34th Infantry Division to recruit a similar unit from volunteers of any US regiment then in Ulster. William Orlando Darby was delighted for it was just what his experience as a cavalryman and staff officer – as well as his enthusiasm – suited him.

The criteria he looked for were much the same as his predecessors sought in selecting for the commandos and airborne forces: physical fitness and general toughness, courage and self-discipline, good marksmanship and fieldcraft, the ability to swim and map read and, ideally, some experience of mountain climbing and small boat handling as well. Because Darby wanted a good cross-section of experts in ordnance, signals, navigation, mechanical repair and maintenance and other specialist skills, he did not just recruit from the infantry but from assorted other army corps as well, luring them with the promise of adventure and 'first crack at the Hun'.

Unfortunately, the Rangers did not have a happy war. Their first experience of battle was during Operation Torch but they were decimated in Sicily and particularly during the battle to break out of the Anzio beachhead a few months later. They were reduced from five to two battalions. The survivors played a crucial role as pathfinders on D-Day, though, while a new sixth battalion fought in the Pacific, but they were all disbanded at the end of the war – temporarily, as events transpired.

The last of the Anglo-American elite forces, the US Marine Corps, has a long history dating back to its formation by Order of Congress on 10 November 1775 that cannot be recounted here. The Corps fought with distinction from 1941–45, particularly in the 'island hopping' campaign against the Japanese in the Pacific.

Some details of its more recent campaigns and battles are given later. However, mention must be made of the USMC's four wartime parachute battalions. Even though one of them saw no action at all and the other three did not make a single combat drop, they saw heavy fighting on Guadalcanal, Bougainville and Choiscul and are included here because they were the precursors of today's 'Recons' – Marine Reconnaissance Units – who are also parachute-trained and form another elite within an existing elite.

Specific mention should also be made of the First Special Service Force, even though it bears no relationship to the modern US Army Special Forces – the 'Green Berets' – which are a post-war phenomenon. This was a joint US-Canadian unit raised in June 1942 from backwoodsmen and trackers under Lieutenant-Colonel Robert Frederick (later commander of the 17th Airborne Division) and tasked with sabotage operations in mountain and arctic conditions although it was never properly deployed in this role. Nick-named the 'Devil's Brigade', it saw action in Italy and southern France during 1943–44 before being disbanded. The experience it gained was particularly useful when Canada began organizing its current Special Service Force in 1968.

Since the sweeping German Blitzkrieg of 1940 left the occupied nations with little opportunity to form similar elite units for special missions, and we have already mentioned the Free French and Belgian units in the SAS, it just remains to look briefly at the Soviet Union. Russia, as we saw at the beginning, was an early exponent of airborne warfare and today has the largest paratroop force in the world.

The first Russian parachute unit was formed in Leningrad in 1931 and by 1933 had been expanded to the size of a brigade with glider-borne troops as well as paras. The first full-scale parachute drop in history – other than in exercises – occurred in November 1939 at the beginning of the Winter War with Finland. Even though it was not particularly successful, further expansion followed so that by the end of 1940 there were six full brigades. Despite an acute shortage of suitable aircraft, when Germany invaded the Soviet Union in June 1941 five European corps were in the process of being formed, each of three brigades, with a further brigade stationed in the Far East. The principal use made of parachute forces during what the Russians call the 'Great Patriotic War' was in support of partisan brigades behind the German lines. Although generally poorly planned and coordinated, these attacks tied down large numbers of German security troops guarding supply centres and escorting convoys. The two large-scale airborne operations – near Vyazma in January 1942 and Kanev in September 1943 – were total disasters with almost the entire air landing force being wiped out in each case. For the remainder of the war the airborne brigades acted as ordinary infantry. Their lack of success can be attributed more to poor equipment, training and leadership than to lack of courage or conviction among the troops, 196 of whom were awarded the Hero of the Soviet Union medal.

Finally we come to the Soviet Naval Infantry, equivalent of the British Royal Marines and US Marine Corps. These have a long history dating back to the days of Tsar Peter the Great and during the Second World War were expanded to a staggering 350,000 men organized in 40 brigades and a number of smaller units. They carried out numerous small-scale landings behind German lines and four full-scale amphibious assaults during 1943–44, two on the Kerch peninsula, one at Novorossiysk on the Black Sea and one at Moon Sound in the Baltic. Generally the Naval Infantry were also employed as ordinary infantry, though, and they were disbanded in 1947 – though only for a short time.

From these varied beginnings have emerged the elite forces of the world as we know them today.

UNITED KINGDOM

The United Kingdom is a small country with a limited military budget which never stretches far enough, but its soldiers – all volunteers, since National Service was abolished in December 1960 – are widely respected for their professionalism. It often surprises people when they count up and realize that British soldiers, sailors and airmen have fought in more than 50 campaigns since the end of the Second World War, one of which has been running for more than 20 years in Northern Ireland, of course. But despite other obligations in places as far flung as Hong Kong and Belize, the British armed forces are principally dedicated to the service of the North Atlantic Treaty Organisation (NATO), and their main theatre of operations if a confrontation ever occurred with the Warsaw Pact would be in Europe.

For this reason the bulk of the front-line regiments and squadrons are normally stationed in West Germany while the Royal Navy's main role is in the North Sea and North Atlantic. However, their ability to respond quickly and flexibly anywhere in the world was clearly shown by their rapid deployment to the Falklands in 1982, while a naval task force was also deployed to protect international shipping during the 1980–88 Gulf War between Iran and Iraq. In recent years the British armed forces have, inevitably, also been deeply involved in the war against international terrorism, and in this role the Special Air Service Regiment is acknowledged to reign supreme.

The Special Air Service Regiments

It is invidious to make distinctions between the many fine, fit, brave and skilled officers and men in the British or any other army, but the three SAS Regiments demand the highest standards of all and while those volunteers who fail to pass their rigorous selection tests may feel disappointed, none can feel ashamed because to be accepted for the course is in itself an accolade. The SAS – or 'Sass' as it is pronounced in the army, without the definite article – nevertheless managed to remain largely out of the public eye until 11 minutes in May 1980 focused the world's attention on the force and some of its more esoteric abilities.

On 5 May, concealed television cameras revealed 'live' to an enthralled audience a situation which would have done credit to a thriller film and which has, of course, been imitated in fiction many times subsequently. On the balcony at the front of the white, colonnaded façade of the Iranian Embassy in Princes Gate, London, suddenly materialized the sinister figures of a number of black-garbed, masked and hooded men carrying automatic weapons and grenade launchers. Since the previous Wednesday, 24 men and women including three Britons, had been held hostage by masked gunmen demanding the release of 91 political prisoners held in Iran by the fanatical Ayatollah Khomeini's regime. Quite how they expected to achieve their aims remains a puzzle because the British government had no influence over that of Iran at the time – almost the reverse in fact!

The police stood by the usual 'rules of engagement' in hostage situations, which state that military action may not be taken until all other avenues of discussion have proved cul de sacs or until the terrorists actually kill one or more of their victims. The SAS, although on standby alert, could not be involved other than in an advisory capacity until one of these criteria was met. However, they did plant microphones, dropping them on cables down chimneys, so they could accurately locate where the hostages were being held and where each terrorist was stationed. Any noise the team from the 22nd Special Air Service Regiment (22 SAS) made while on the roof of the building was masked by the sound of pneumatic drills from nearby 'roadworks'.

Tension built. The terrorists, led by a man only identified as 'Oan', had demanded a meeting

Heckler & Koch MP5

The principal German military smallarms manufacturer since the Second World War, Heckler & Koch, was founded in 1948 and began making the army's G3 rifle in 1956 shortly after the Federal Republic was admitted to NATO. This caused a row at the time because the rifle was an improved copy of the CETME design developed from war-time plans by Nazi engineers who had sought refuge from Allied justice in General Franco's Spain! H&K subsequently developed the MP5 (MP derives from Maschinen-Pistole) sub-machine gun which uses many components of the G3 and the heavier HK21 machine gun, saving production costs.

MP5SD1 which does not have a stock at all; the MP5SD2 which has a fixed plastic butt; and the MP5SD3 which has the metal stock. Finally there is a miniaturized version only 325 mm long, the MP5KA1, which is specially designed for covert operations since it can be concealed almost as easily as a pistol. There is no stock, the barrel is almost non-existent and there is a small hand grip just behind and below the muzzle. Range is no more than that of a pistol but the automatic fire capability is useful in counter-terrorist operations.

All MP5 variants are chambered to 9 mm calibre (with a smaller version just being introduced) and have straight or curved 15- or 30-

There is a whole family of MP5s, the MP5A2 being the most common. This has a plastic butt in line with the barrel, a pistol grip and the magazine receiver in front of the trigger. The MP5A3 used by the SAS during the embassy siege is identical except that it has a retractable tubular metal stock, reducing the weapon's overall length and making it especially suitable for use in confined spaces. There are three silenced versions: the

round box magazines. A delayed blowback firing mechanism gives a cyclic rate of fire of up to 800 rounds per minute (rpm). A useful feature is a selector switch enabling the weapon to be fired single-shot, in bursts of two to four rounds, or fully automatic. The sights on the basic MP5A2 are calibrated to 440 yards (400 m) but normal effective range is more like 220 yards (200 m), and even less with the silenced versions.

TOP The miniaturized MP5K. **ABOVE** The silenced MP5SD2.

with representatives of other Middle Eastern countries and subsequent safe conduct to a plane at Heathrow Airport. The demands went unanswered since you do not negotiate with terrorists (even if you pretend to): you just wear them down until they finally realize they cannot win. Then one of the prisoners, assistant press attaché Abbas Lavasani, who was a devoted follower of Khomeini, somehow managed to get to a telephone. The terrorists shot him out of hand. Sir David McNee, Commissioner of Police in charge of the negotiations, rushed the senior Iman of the London Central Mosque to the phone to plead for moderation. 'Why should we wait any longer?', the terrorist leader demanded. Sounds of further shots were heard, then a body was dumped outside the embassy's front door. It was assumed that a second hostage had been killed and the decision was taken: send in the SAS. (In fact the firing had been a bluff and the body was actually Lavasani's, but no-one on the outside could have known that at the time.)

The SAS operation had been meticulously rehearsed. Three teams each of four men, were deployed, one entering the front of the building from the adjoining balcony next door, one abseiling down on ropes from the roof to smash through windows in the rear, and the third bursting in through a wall from next door, the bricks having been carefully removed leaving only the facing plaster in place. In order to gain entrance they used frame charges, following through with stun grenades (colloquially known in the army as 'flash bangs') and tear gas. Their principal weapon – a favourite in the SAS and many other counter-terrorist units – was the German Heckler & Koch MP5 sub-machine gun, popularly known as the 'Hockler'. The members of the assault party were dressed in black overalls over kevlar body armour, with black balaclava anti-flash helmets and gasmasks. In the street outside, police marksmen from D11 – the 'Blue Berets' – waited for targets of opportunity,

Masked SAS men on the front balcony of the Iranian Embassy.

Browning Hi-Power automatic pistols at the ready.

At 7.26 pm on that warm early summer evening, reasoning that the terrorists would be less likely to expect an assault while it was still daylight, the SAS teams went into action. As the first pair of troopers reached the balcony at the front, a second pair abseiled down to the first floor balcony at the rear. Then came a hitch. One of the men in the third pair got his rope snagged. This meant that the troopers below him could not use their frame charges without injuring him, so they had to simply kick in the windows, hurling their 'flash bangs' which cause disorientation but do not generally otherwise harm. As the second pair of troopers swung in through the first floor windows at the rear, 'Oan', who had been temporarily distracted by a carefully timed telephone call, ran to the landing and raised his automatic pistol. Police Constable Trevor Lock, a member of the Diplomatic Protection Group who was among the hostages, flung himself at the gunman, distracting his aim until an SAS trooper shot him.

Meanwhile another hostage, BBC sound engineer Simeon Harris, had fled to the front of the building. Throwing back the curtains, he was astounded to see what he thought was a 'frogman' on the balcony. The SAS man urgently motioned him to move back and four seconds later a frame charge exploded, showering the room with glass, and four soldiers dived into the building. Simultaneously, the third team broke through the adjoining wall.

On the second floor above the 15 male hostages (who had been separated from the women) listened in horror to the explosions and gunfire. When the attack had begun there had been only one guard present in the room, but now two more terrorists ran in and began shooting at them. One Iranian official was killed and two more wounded. But then, as if realizing the futility of their actions, the men threw down their guns and attempted to mingle with the hostages.

The deception did not save them – the SAS shot to kill. Only one of the six terrorists, who had been guarding the women at the back of the building, was allowed to surrender. The whole operation had taken 11 minutes and seconds later the relieved hostages began emerging, hustled to safety by the soldiers because several small fires had broken out. It was a miniature classic of an operation, watched by astonished millions as it actually happened, and for really the first time the general public started demanding to know who these SAS 'supermen' were.

The present-day SAS, which consists of three regiments, one Regular and two Territorial, came into being in a rather odd fashion. The wartime 1st SAS Brigade was disbanded in October 1945 but within a few months the War Office (now the Ministry of Defence) decided that there would, after all, be a need for such a force in the postwar world. They reactivated a Territorial Army regiment, 'The Artists' Rifles', as the 21st Special Air Service Regiment (Artists) – (Volunteers) in 1946. Then, in 1951, three years after the start of the Malayan Emergency, Brigadier Michael Calvert arrived. The former CO of 1st SAS Brigade 1944–45, he quickly formed a new volunteer counter-insurgency unit called the Malayan Scouts (SAS). This rapidly grew to a strength of three battalions (which the SAS calls squadrons), one composed of volunteers from other units, one from 21 SAS and one from Rhodesian volunteers. A year later it was re-designated 22nd Special Air Service Regiment and became an established part of the regular army. In 1956 the Rhodesians returned home and were replaced by a New Zealand squadron which included many Maoris and Fijians, all tough fighters. Subsequently a second TA regiment was raised, 23 SAS, broadly based in the north of England while 21 covers the south.

The situation in Malaya was complex and needed careful handling. After the war many local guerrillas who had fought against the Japanese started a campaign to try to establish a communist regime. Operating from camps deep in the jungle, between 1948 and 1950 they had killed more than 1,300 people and the British infantry battalions stationed in Singapore had made precious little headway against them. Calvert inaugurated what was then a revolutionary 'hearts and minds' campaign to win over the local population and deny the guerrillas their support. The SAS men, alongside Gurkhas and Royal Marines, not only fought the communists on their home ground, but also built roads, bridges, clinics and schools while education officers fluent in local dialects preached the principles of democracy. Victory did not come overnight – the emergency lasted until 1960 – but the campaign was eventually successful and has become a model for subsequent operations of similar nature. What might have happened in Indo-China had the French and, later, the Americans tried harder to adopt similar tactics remains speculation.

The task accomplished and many useful lessons learned, not least the techniques of parachuting into treetops and then abseiling on ropes down to the jungle floor, 22 SAS next found itself embroiled in a very different campaign in the pro-British Persian Gulf Sultanate of Muscat and Oman. Here, in the mid-1950s, dissidents supported by the powerful state of Saudi Arabia had been stirring up trouble which the Omani's own Trucial Scouts were unable to suppress. In 1958 the SAS were sent in, and launched a series of surprise attacks on the rebel stronghold on the Jabal Akhdar plateau and in the surrounding mountains, and in three months had suppressed the rebellion. They would return later, but in the meantime trouble had again broken out in the Far East, this time in Borneo.

Although Gurkhas bore the brunt of the fighting during what has subsequently come to be called the 'Brunei Confrontation', in which President Sukarno of Indonesia tried by force to unite Brunei and Sarawak into a new 'communist' state, the SAS was involved from 1963–65 when a coup deposed Sukarno, known to the troops as 'the mad doctor'. Similar tactics to those employed in Malaya worked particularly well with a population which did not want to be ruled from Peking (now Beijing). For the SAS it was now back to the Middle East, first to Aden (now North and South Yemen), then Oman once more in the early 1970s when a mere 10 troopers routed a force of more than 250 rebels at the battle of Mirbat. While in Oman this time the SAS recruited and trained a potent force of national levies, the Firqats, fierce local tribesmen who took with delight to the form of irregular warfare in which the SAS excels and who, by the end of 1975, had brought the country back under the Sultan's control.

In the interim the SAS had become heavily involved in the British army's running battle with those who are fighting for a united Irish Roman Catholic republic. Unlike other army regiments on tour in the Province, who operate openly in the streets, in uniform, the SAS operates clandestinely. Its frequently long-haired personnel, wearing donkey jackets and wellingtons and speaking a perfect dialect, form the 'eyes and ears' of the Intelligence Corps, listening quietly in pubs and feeding back snippets of information which, when pieced together with others, can reveal the hideout of a wanted terrorist or a cache of hidden arms and explosives. This is dangerous, nerve-shredding work with death or mutilation never further away than a single wrong word, and details will remain under wraps for decades – indeed, some will almost certainly never be made public.

The SAS also operates as part of the border patrol network, although the government did not admit this until 1974, five years after the current 'Troubles' began. Teams of four men – the SAS's normal tactical unit – may lie hidden in ambush for days, hardly moving in well-camouflaged hides, enduring filth, damp, cold and meagre uncooked rations until a man or group of men attempt to slip across the border.

Then they strike, and the incident reaches the newspapers a few days later as a random interception by a border patrol from a totally different regiment. Nor are known terrorists who flee abroad safe from 'Sass' as the much-publicized executions in Gibraltar proved. The SAS hates such publicity, for if 'Who Dares Wins' is their motto, secrecy is their watchword. Unfortunately, but inevitably, the regiment came into the public eye again during the Falklands' campaign.

At 4.15 in the morning of 15 May 1982, Griff Evans, a sheep farmer in the small community on Pebble Island (off the coast of West Falkland), was woken by the sound of explosions. Peering through a window he saw the whole night sky brilliantly illuminated by exploding flares, ammunition and oil drums from the nearby airstrip which the occupying Argentine troops were using as an alternative to Port Stanley. As Griff made his anxious wife a cup of coffee, the couple were completely unaware that their house was screened against Argentine retaliation by a 16-man troop from 'D' Squadron, 22 SAS. A second troop had placed explosive charges in the 11 aircraft on the strip while a third stood by in reserve. Then the destroyer HMS Glamorgan brought her guns into play, her shots zeroed in by an artillery observer accompanying the SAS teams. The result was the destruction of all the Argentine aircraft and the radar installation which could have been used to help guide aircraft attacking the British Task Force. It was the first indication that Argentine commander General Menendez had that British forces had arrived in the Falklands, although he was obviously aware that the more easterly island of South Georgia had already been recaptured, along with the submarine Santa Fe.

The men of 'D' and 'G' Squadrons played a major part in the liberation of the Falklands, providing reconnaissance reports for the Commandos and Paras who landed after them and infiltrating Argentine positions at night to kill

SAS trooper, his eyes obscured by the censor, during an exercise in the Brecon Beacons.

sentries, reducing the opposing troops' already shaky morale. Inevitably, they took casualties too, 19 men from 'D' Troop being killed in a helicopter crash and the popular commander of Mountain Troop, Captain John Hamilton, dying while giving covering fire for the other three men in his patrol, an act of valour for which he was awarded a posthumous Victoria Cross. Other SAS teams were reportedly active in mainland Argentina, attacking airfields, although this has never been confirmed. The same is true of persistent reports that the SAS were involved in Afghanistan where their task would have been observation and evaluation of Soviet tactics, particularly those of Russia's own elite Spetsnaz forces. Such operations must, of necessity, remain secret for many years, but over the last decade many hitherto unknown details of SAS recruitment, training and organization have been made public and it is worth looking at these in depth because they serve as a model for other elite forces around the world.

Unlike the elite forces of some nations, the SAS does not recruit directly from the public but only from within the existing regiments and corps of the British army, particularly from the Parachute Regiment and the Brigade of Guards which are already elite forces in their own right. Even then, not all those who apply are admitted to the rigorous selection course, held twice a year, because the SAS looks for a particular type of person. There is no disgrace in having an application refused because a man can be a perfectly good soldier, competent, skilled and reliable, but just lack that psychological make-up which the SAS needs. A primary requisite is self-confidence, but not cockiness or an insubordinate attitude. Coupled to this there has to be drive, determination to excel and, in many ways even more important, to endure in the face of physical hardship, pain and severe mental stress. Physical and mental strength and discipline are thus essential. The initial selection procedure is designed to test these qualities to

breaking point for in an operational four-man team, each individual has to have total, uncompromising faith in his 'mates'.

The selection course, originally designed by Malayan veteran John Woodhouse in the 1950s, is constantly being revised but typically lasts for between three and four weeks. The first half emphasizes physical fitness and map reading with long marches in small groups through the rugged Brecon mountains of Wales. This is designed to bring each recruit up to a common standard. Once the men – their numbers already whittled down by either voluntary or compulsory withdrawal from the course – reach the necessary standard, and have proved that they can stand the pace and navigate accurately in fog or at night using just a map and a compass, they are broken up into smaller groups for even more intensive practice, and are finally sent out individually to complete set tasks within a time limit. A 'sickener' to test their stamina is always thrown in at some point, the recruit arriving at his destination only to be told he has to return to his starting point. This finishes off many aspirants even when they know beforehand that they will have to face the test at some point. The end of the course is 'celebrated' by a gruelling 40 mile (64 km) hike over the mountains carrying a rifle and 55 lb (25 kg) bergen rucksack, an ordeal which has to be completed in 20 hours. Even at the end of all this the surviving 10 to 20 per cent of the original intake are still not members of the SAS, but have to undergo a further 14 weeks of more specialized training.

If this initial emphasis on cross-country marching and navigation seems strange, it has a very logical purpose. The principal task of the SAS in time of war is reconnaissance and sabotage deep behind enemy lines, and each man has to be capable of fending for himself during the approach to the objective and subsequent withdrawal, which could conceivably last weeks. Under such circumstances there is always, of course, the possibility of capture and for this reason the men are taught to memorize map references rather than write them down, and to fold their maps carefully so as to avoid revealing the locality they are interested in, or where they have come from.

The greatly reduced intake of new recruits now spends seven weeks in what is called 'general' training in the SAS's standard operating procedures (SOPs). They learn how to work together in four-man teams, practising reconnaissance, sabotage and ambush techniques and honing the basic skills of first aid, fieldcraft and marksmanship which they will have already learned in their parent regiment or corps. They are also taught how to resist interrogation under very realistic conditions which stop only just short of actual physical torture. Then follow three weeks of combat survival training in which the men learn how to live off the land. This goes

SAS men in action with FN 7.62 mm rifles (below) and (opposite) displaying some of their equipment including high altitude parachute, scuba, mountain, arctic and tropical kit.

much deeper than finding out how to snare a rabbit or 'tickle' a fish, for survival in the field does not just involve eating and drinking, it depends on avoiding detection by the enemy, so the careful siting and camouflage of a 'hide' is just as important. At the end of this phase of training recruits are sent out into some region of rugged countryside equipped with just a knife and a box of matches and have to survive for five days while avoiding detection by the instructors hunting them down. This is part of the 'escape and evasion' training.

Finally comes what most recruits consider the 'fun' part of the course. It is also the most expensive, which is why the army leaves it until last, saving unnecesary costs by ensuring that the surviving recruits are almost certain to make the grade. This is parachute training at Brize Norton, the Royal Air Force station in Oxfordshire.

Trained members of the Parachute Regiment do not have to undergo the basic part of the course but instead help the instructors, although they do have to take the seven jumps – three of them with full equipment and one of them at night – which are the final criteria for admission to 'the Regiment', (As mentioned earlier, there are in fact three regiments, 22 SAS composed of Regulars and 21 and 23 SAS which are part of the Territorial Army; volunteers for the latter two regiments have exactly the same training as the Regulars but it is spread over a period of up to three years because it has to be fitted in with the demands of the men's civilian jobs. The TA has long since lived down its 'Dad's Army' image and its men are just as tough and professional as the Regulars, even though they often have to make do with handed-down vehicles and weapons.)

For men of any of the regiments, now, at last, comes award of the coveted beige beret with its famous winged dagger badge, but even so they are still only on probation and will remain so for a further nine months (longer in the TA) while they learn more specialized skills and decide, depending on aptitude, inclination and ability, which type of Troop they will finally join.

Each of the three SAS regiments divided into four squadrons, known as 'Sabre' squadrons and lettered 'A', 'B', 'D' and 'G'. In addition, 22 and 23 SAS both have separate signals squadrons. A regiment averages about 600-plus men including headquarters and supporting services and each Sabre squadron is divided into four Troops of 16 men. These are Boat, Air, Mountain and Mobility Troops. The men of Boat Troop undergo much the same training as the Royal Marines' Special Boat Squadron and learn canoeing and small boat handling, offshore and inshore navigation, sub-aqua swimming using either scuba or oxygen rebreathing sets, and the techniques of beach reconnaissance and underwater demolition. The men of Air Troop learn advanced parachuting techniques in-

cluding high altitude/low opening (HALO) and high altitude/high opening (HAHO) jumping. Both these techniques allow them to be dropped – normally from an RAC C-130 Hercules – at 30,000 ft (9,000 m) or so several miles from their objective by day or by night.

Mountain Troop men train alongside the Royal Marines' Mountain & Arctic Warfare Cadre in skiing, rock and ice climbing, mountain navigation and high altitude survival. They also learn how to dig snowholes, burrowing into the snow to create artificial caves both for shelter from the wind and concealment from the enemy, breathing by poking a hole through the 'ceiling' with a ski stick. Finally, Mobility Troop learns how to drive, maintain and repair the wide range of vehicles used not just by the British army but by those of other countries as well, and many of its personnel reach international rally driving standards. (All members of the SAS routinely learn to use and maintain the full range of NATO and Warsaw Pact smallarms too, as do the special forces of other nations, of course.)

Training does not stop here, for every man in the SAS is constantly sharpening his expertise. A normal 'tour' with the Regiment is three years after which a man will usually (but not necessarily) return to his parent outfit, thereby spreading SAS skills gradually throughout the whole army. During these three years many men gravitate from Troop to Troop to increase their knowledge and capabilities yet further. Those with a gift for languages may attend the army's language school at Beaconsfield in Buckinghamshire and some of them will later join army intelligence, or 'I' Corps (often known as 'eye-spy corps'!) Some will spend a period with the Army Air Corps learning how to fly fixed-wing aircraft and helicopters. Other men specialize in the counter-terrorist role and learn the techniques of entering and fighting inside houses at the Regiment's special training centre at Hereford, its headquarters. The Regiment also maintains close links with the special forces of other friendly nations, particularly in the USA, Australia and New Zealand but also with the Belgian 1st Parachute Regiment which is descended from the wartime SAS and with West Germany's GSG9, and there is a great deal of cross-pollination of ideas and techniques as well as carousing in the Mess.

The Parachute Regiment

The three SAS regiments maintain particularly close links with The Parachute Regiment from which a large proportion of their personnel are drawn. At the time of writing the Regiment consists of three Regular battalions headquartered at Aldershot – 1, 2 and 3 Para – and three Territorial battalions – 4, 10 and 15 Para. With the end of the Second World War there was an inevitable rundown in the size of Britain's airborne forces, the 1st Airborne Division being dis-

On exercise in West Germany, a light infantryman with a 7.62 mm General Purpose Machine-Gun, popularly known as a 'Gimpy'.

banded in 1945 and the 6th in 1948 leaving just a single brigade which was given the number 16 to commemorate the two earlier formations.

The 16th Independent Parachute Brigade Group, to give it its full title, saw a great deal of action during the 1950s, one squadron operating alongside the SAS in Malaya and others serving in Egypt or in Cyprus in the battle against EOKA terrorists. In November 1956 the brigade's 3rd Battalion parachuted in to capture the airfield at Port Said in advance of the Anglo-French-Israeli invasion of Egypt designed to retake the Suez Canal which President Nasser had nationalized. Unfortunately, this invasion provoked a worldwide outcry and the occupying forces were compelled by the United Nations to withdraw, leading indirectly to two later wars between Egypt and Israel. The brigade was also involved in supporting King Hussein of

Jordan when trouble erupted in Lebanon and Iraq in 1958, as well as in Aden, Borneo, British Guiana and Anguilla. Inevitably, the brigade was involved in peacekeeping duties in Northern Ireland from 1969 onwards.

On 30 January 1972 an incident occurred which gave the Paras much unwanted and unjustified publicity. The 1st Battalion was on duty in Londonderry tasked with controlling an illegal protest march. A group of youths began bombarding them with stones and CS riot gas canisters, then snipers from the Provisional wing of the Irish Republican Army (PIRA, generally just known by the army as 'Provos') began shooting at them from a block of flats. The Paras returned fire and 13 men in the crowd were killed. The IRA accused them of firing indiscriminately at 'innocent women and children' and the incident has subsequently entered history as 'Bloody Sunday'. In fact, of course, if the Paras had indeed fired indiscriminately the carnage from their 7.62 mm self-loading rifles (SLRs), each with a 20-round magazine, would have been far higher. The IRA exacted revenge on 27 August 1979, ambushing a convoy of trucks at Warrenpoint and killing 16 of the regiment's men, an incident overshadowed by the assassination of Lord Louis Mountbatten on the same day.

By this time 16 Parachute Brigade no longer existed, having been disbanded by a cost-conscious government on 31 March 1977 and all that was left was a single airborne battalion in what was then known as 6 Field Force, the other two battalions serving purely in an ordinary infantry role. Each battalion consists of six companies: headquarters, support and four rifle. The army fortunately maintained airborne training by rotating the three battalions and when Margaret Thatcher became Prime Minister in 1979 one of the first things she did was authorize two airborne battalions, 2 and 3 Para, with all necessary aircraft and equipment. These formed part of 5 Infantry Brigade from the beginning of 1982 while 1 Para was back on duty in Northern

OPPOSITE British special forces have had some of their most notable successes in jungles from Malaya to Belize, and are seen here with a 'Gimpy' on its sustained fire tripod.

Ireland – to their great chagrin for it was 2 and 3 Para, seconded to 3 Commando Brigade, Royal Marines, who reaped glory in the Falklands.

Lacking at the time an equivalent of the American Rapid Deployment Force, it was a tribute to the British armed forces, to the mercantile marine and to the resolution of the government that the Task Force was on its way to the South Altantic within seven days of the Argentine invasion on 2 April 1982. 3 Para, on leave for Easter and with one of its officers on his honeymoon, was recalled in record time and sailed aboard the liner SS Canberra on the 9th, followed by 2 Para and all support teams and equipment on the SS Norland on the 26th. It was actually 2 Para which had the distinction of being the first major unit ashore at San Carlos on 21 May, although SAS and SBS reconnaissance teams had been operating on East Falkland for some time.

The SAS had reported an Argentine force of approximately battalion strength occupying Darwin and Goose Green settlements to the south of San Carlos and the Task Force commander, Rear Admiral 'Sandy' Woodward, ordered 2 Para to take this out so as to secure the ground forces' right flank. The battalion moved off across the mountains and was in position on 27 May. Unknown to them, though, the Argentine garrison had been reinforced by two more battalions so the Paras would be attacking at odds of one to three – the exact reverse of the ratio normally recommended for an assault on an enemy in prepared positions. Moreover, although 2 Para had an unusually high quota of 7.62 mm General Purpose Machine Guns ('Gimpys') because it had been preparing for a tour in Belize at the time of the Argentine invasion, its only support weapons were a mere three 105 mm Light Guns and two 81 mm mortars.

The battalion moved off from its start line at 3 am on the 28th, led by its commander, Lieutenant-Colonel 'H' Jones, and immediately ran

ABOVE A candidate for the Parachute Regiment slogs his way through the arduous assault course.

OPPOSITE They have to be prepared for all situations, and all climates.

into stiff opposition from well-sited .50 calibre heavy machine-guns and artillery. Nevertheless, by midday the Paras were in a strong position although 'A' Company was pinned down by a couple of strong machine-gun positions. It was this point that 'H' led a flanking attack to eliminate the obstacles; he was hit several times and died shortly afterwards, but the Argentine positions were overrun. Colonel Jones was subsequently awarded the Victoria Cross for an action very much up to British airborne forces' tradition, although it was subsequently questioned whether it was the proper role of a battalion CO to lead such an assault in person. Command was assumed by Major Chris Keeble and by nightfall 2 Para had taken Darwin and surrounded Goose Green despite an air attack by four Argentine aircraft. Keeble, worried about potential casualties among the civilian population if the Paras launched a direct assault, sent in a prisoner with a surrender demand in the morning and two Argentine NCOs emerged with a white flag. A Spanish-speaking Royal Marines' officer, Captain Rod Bell, accompanied them back into Goose Green to meet the garrison commander, Air Vice-Commodore Wilson Pedrozo. At one o'clock the Argentines laid down their arms and lined up to surrender. The Paras were astounded – 'gobsmacked' in their own words – to find themselves in charge of 1,350 prisoners plus 190 dead and wounded. 2 Para's own casualties were 15 dead and 30 wounded. It was a truly remarkable feat of arms.

Meanwhile, Lieutenant-Colonel Hew Pike's 3 Para had been force-marching overland towards Teal Inlet on the northern coast, which they reached on the 29th. They then moved up to Mount Kent, to the west of the islands' capital, Port Stanley. Here they dug in to await the arrival of artillery support, which was delayed by an acute shortage of helicopters. Their next objective was Mount Longdon, which was heavily defended by the Argentine 7th Infantry Regiment and a number of crack Buzo Tactico troops

– Argentine equivalent of the SAS. The attack finally went in during the night of 11/12 June and it was immediately apparent that the Argentine forces here were not going to give in without a tough fight. Explosions from grenades, rockets and artillery fire rent the night air while deceptively lazy streams of tracer from dozens of machine guns flew through the moonlit sky. A minefield blocked one avenue of approach and the sheet weight of fire made it difficult to get near the well dug-in machine gun nests. One in particular held up the advance until Sergeant Ian McKay of 'B' Company led four of his men in a frontal assault, charging up the hill with blazing SLRs. McKay seemed to lead a charmed life as one after another of his men fell, but he was finally hit just as he reached the parapet. Although he was also killed, his falling body blocked the breech of the machine gun and the rest of his Company was able to capture the position. Like 'H' Jones and John Hamilton, Ian McKay was awarded a well-deserved post-humous Victoria Cross.

With Mount Longdon secured, it was 2 Para's turn again the next night. The objective was Wireless Ridge, one of the last remaining pieces of high ground overlooking Port Stanley. The battalion had been flown in by helicopter following its victory at Goose Green and this time its assault was fully supported by artillery and the light Scorpion and Scimitar tanks of the Blues and Royals. As one observer commented, 'the Paras loved it' as the heavy firepower dislodged one Argentine position after another. Only three of the battalion's men fell during the final assault and when daybreak arrived on 14 June, Keeble's triumphant troops had the literal drop on the disorganized and demoralized Argentine garrison in Port Stanley. Jauntily, wearing their berets instead of their helmets, they sauntered, strolled or ran down the hill, many of them yelling at the tops of their voices, past despondent Argentine soldiers who did not even put up a token resistance. General Menendez formally surrendered later in the afternoon.

In October the following year 5 Infantry Brigade was rechristened 5 Airborne Brigade and entrusted to the command of Brigadier Tony Jeapes, a former CO of 22 SAS. The Falklands' experience had shown the need for a British air-trained rapid deployment force and the brigade currently consists of Nos 2 and 3 Para, No 2 Battalion King Edward VII's Own Gurkha Rifles (The Sirmoor Rifles), a squadron of Fox armoured cars and Scorpion and Scimitar light tanks from the Life Guards, No 7 Field Regiment, Royal Horse Artillery (RHA), No 9 Para Field Squadron, Royal Engineers (RE), Nos 20 and 50 Field Squadrons, RE, No 61 Field Support Squadron, RE, No 23 Field Ambulance, Royal Army Medical Corps (RAMC), No 63 Squadron, Royal Corps of Transport (RCT), No 10 Field Workshop, Royal Electrical and Mechanical Engineers (REME) and No 82 Ordnance Company, Royal Army Ordnance Corps (RAOC). Airlift capability is provided by Nos 47 and 70 Squadrons, RAF, based at Lyneham in Wiltshire, both of which played key roles in providing aid after the Mexico City earthquake in 1985 and during the Ethiopian famine with their C-130 Hercules aircraft. Finally, helicopter support is provided by the Gazelles of 658 Squadron, Army Air Corps.

The modern brigade is therefore a go anywhere, anytime force, ready to respond at short notice to an emergency in any part of the world. No 1 Para is not part of the brigade but instead forms a component in the Allied Command Europe Mobile Force (AMF), a multinational task force specifically trained in arctic warfare and dedicated to demonstrate NATO solidarity in the case of an invasion of Norway.

Parachute training after the arduous initial induction period into the Parachute Regiment comes, as in the SAS, almost as a relief because each man knows that this is the final hurdle before he can wear his 'wings' and the famous 'red' beret. The whole course lasts 23 weeks,

Paras with a Milan anti-tank missile firing post in Norway.

the first seven of which are principally designed to toughen recruits up physically for what is to come later. Actual strength, in the weightlifting sense, is not required although it can come in handy. Stamina, the ability to keep on going when every fibre of the body screams for rest, is far more important – as the recruits soon discover. These seven weeks culminate in a realistic exercise in the Welsh mountains, after which each recruit's performance is examined by a selection committee. Some men are weeded out at this stage, others are given a second chance to prove their mettle and the remainder progress to the second stage of the course. For them the next three weeks involve advanced weapons training although the physical toughening-up continues. There is then a second review board before successful candidates go through to the third stage which involves crossing obstacle courses with some stretches over ropes up to 50 ft above the ground to test confidence, compulsory boxing matches to test aggression and cross-country races carrying various loads. At the end of this, successful recruits are allowed to wear the red beret but still have to earn their parachutist's wings.

Following a further four weeks' instruction in fieldcraft and tactics, recruits are finally sent to Brize Norton where they are taught the correct way to fall and practise controlled drops from a hangar roof and then the tower before they make their first actual drop from a balloon. The British army is one of the last in the world to retain balloons for parachute training but there is an excellent psychological reason for it is actually more difficult to steel yourself to jump from a stationary platform hundreds of feet above the ground than it is from an aircraft. Some candidates balk at this hurdle and are reluctantly eased out of the army or into a different regiment but the survivors go on to complete seven jumps from a Hercules and are then awarded their wings. Apart from the balloon jump, parachute training in other armies follows a very similar pattern.

Gurkhas through the ages: a 10th Gurkha Rifles machine-gunner from 1930 (below) and (opposite) a junior officer and radio operator from the 6th Queen Elizabeth's Own during a modern jungle exercise.

The Gurkhas

The feisty Nepalese hillmen who have formed part of the British army since 1816 are decidedly an elite, respected by all, liked by their allies and feared by their foes. The presence of the 1st Battalion, 7th Duke of Edinburgh's Own Gurkha Rifles (then part of 5 Infantry Brigade) in the Falklands provoked panic among the Argentine conscripts facing them. The reason was the grossly exaggerated horror stories circulating (helped along by propaganda broadcasts from ships in the British Task Force!) about the uses to which the Gurkhas could put their favoured weapon, the kukri. This thick, curved leaf-shaped knife, which comes in a variety of different sizes, is both a useful chopping tool and a much more effective close-combat weapon than a bayonet. Its cutting edge is kept razor sharp and it can inflict hideous

wounds, with the result that many Argentine soldiers feared mutilation if they fell into Gurkha hands. The Gurkhas, of course, do not practise mutilation, being as highly trained and disciplined as anyone in the British army, but these fears helped spur the Argentine surrender when the battalion moved up alongside the 2nd Battalion, Scots Guards, to take Mount Tumbledown and Mount William overlooking Port Stanley. While the Guards had a tough fight for the former feature, the defenders of the latter simply ran away once they realized who they were facing!

Gurkhas are all volunteers and the young 17-year-olds who flock from their remote villages to the recruiting depots at Pokhara and Dharan each year employ all sorts of tricks to gain acceptance, including falsifying their ages and drinking several pints of water to put on weight before

Gurkhas have a fearsome reputation, but their professionalism is also renowned. ABOVE Map reading exercises are an essential part of navigation anywhere, but especially in the jungle. OPPOSITE The Sterling sub-machine-gun, being shorter than an ordinary rifle, is ideal for the close-quarters work that jungle warfare entails.

their medical examination. Nevertheless, there are many disappointed faces and even tears at the end of the initial selection, for the six battalions in the Brigade of Gurkhas – now known as Gurkha Field Force – can only accept approximately one in 15 of the young hopefuls. Many, rejected first time round, try again the following year, while others opt to join the Indian army.

Apart from height and weight, physical stamina, general intelligence; literacy and numeracy are among the criteria for acceptance, for service in the Brigade is regarded as a privilege rather than a right. Apart from the obvious incentives of decent pay and an opportunity for travel which would otherwise be out of the question, the youngsters are motivated by the glamorized stories their elders tell of action in North Africa and Italy during the Second World War or of Malaya, Borneo and other campaigns sub-

sequently, for Gurkhas have fought just about everywhere the British army has been this century.

The jubilant few accepted at the end of each induction period are flown to Hong Kong and established in the depot at Sek Kong in the New Territories where they will spend the next 32 weeks undergoing basic training. This is longer than normal because the recruits have to learn about the outside world as well as eating heartily to build up their weight and strength and learning codes of conduct and discipline totally foreign to them. Those who endure this period – and there are very few voluntary dropouts – go on for a further eight weeks' training in small-arms use, fieldcraft, navigation and, in particular, internal security duties because the Brigade's principal task in peacetime is the defence of Hong Kong against smugglers and illegal immigrants. The initial period of service is four years (and a soldier does not get home leave until he has served three) but there is fierce competition for promotion to NCO status and the opportunity to stay on longer, since 15 years is the minimum qualifying period for a pension.

From a quarter of a million men in 55 battalions at the end of the Second World War the Gurkhas had shrunk to ten regiments by the time India

ABOVE Gurkhas do not just train for jungle warfare – these Canadian prairies could just as easily be Asiatic steppes.

BELOW A night reconnaissance patrol in the New Territories of Hong Kong.

and Pakistan gained independence in 1947, after which four regiments remained part of the British army and the remainder joined the Indian army. The current line-up is six battalions in four understrength regiments, two each in the 2nd King Edward's Own and the 7th Duke of Edinburgh's Own and one apiece in the 6th Queen Elizabeth's Own and 10th Princess Mary's Own. In addition the Gurkhas have their own Signals, Engineer and Transport Regiments, making the Brigade completely self-contained. The battalions are rotated on a regular basis, one being stationed at Church Cookham as part of 5 Airborne Brigade and frequently providing guards and a band for ceremonial duties

Gurkhas patrolling an inland waterway in Malaysia – hunting for drugs and illegal immigrants are amongst their most important tasks.

at Buckingham Palace. While stationed in the UK, many Gurkhas also take advantage of the parachute training offered at Brize Norton although there is no longer an independent Gurkha parachute battalion. The others are based in Hong Kong, four active, one training and one seconded to Brunei. Gurkhas have also seen action in recent years in Belize as well as the Falklands. Apart from their kukris and smart brimmed hats or ceremonial 'pillboxes', they are uniformed and equipped just like the rest of the British army. Despite their small numbers – currently just above 8,000 – they remain one of the most formidable fighting forces in the world, particularly in jungle warfare.

The Royal Marine Commandos, Special Boat Squadron and Mountain & Arctic Warfare Cadre

While the army Commando battalions were disbanded shortly after the end of the Second World War, three of the Royal Marine units were retained – Nos 40, 42 and 45 Commandos – plus a number of smaller specialized units. No 41 Commando was revived to take part in the Korean War 1950–52, disbanded, reformed in 1961 and finally disbanded for the third time in 1968. Subsequently the three Commandos, each approximately 650 men strong, have been involved in Malaya, Borneo, Uganda, Kenya, Tanganyika, Egypt, Cyprus and, of course, Northern Ireland and the Falklands. In fact, it was Royal Marines who saw first action against the Argentine invaders when they landed on East Falkland on 2 April 1982. Present on the island was a tiny force of 92 Marines and Royal Naval personnel from the ice patrol vessel *HMS Endurance*. They miraculously succeeded in beating off the first attack which was spearheaded by 150 members of the Buzo Tactico, but when the Argentines started landing LVTP-7 Amtrack amphibious armoured personnel

carriers the islands' Governor, Rex Hunt, ordered them to lay down their arms to prevent civilian casualties.

There was also a small party of two dozen Royal Marines on the remote island of South Georgia when the Argentines landed there the following day. They succeeded in disabling two helicopters and holing the Argentine corvette Guerrico with an anti-tank missile before they were surrounded and forced to surrender. Retribution was swift. Three weeks later a scratch force of 75 Commandos, SAS and Special Boat Squadron personnel landed by helicopter from the destroyer *HMS Antrim* (which provided fire support) and quickly overwhelmed the Argentine garrison which surrendered on 26 April.

Nos 40, 42 and 45 Commando form the principal component of 3 Commando Brigade which at the time of the Falklands' conflict was commanded by Brigadier Julian Thompson. The Brigade is commmpletely self-contained and includes two army units, 29 Commando Regiment, Royal Artillery, with 105 mm guns and 59 Independent Commando Squadron, Royal Engineers. It has its own helicopter squadron, 3 CBAS, equipped with Gazelle utility and Lynx anti-tank aircraft, while the Fleet Air Arm provides logistic support and troop-carrying ability with the larger Sea King HC4s of 845 and 846 Squadrons. In addition there is the Commando Logistic Regiment which provides support to 3 Commando Brigade and all other Royal Marine units, 539 Assault Squadron and an Air Defence Troop equipped with Blowpipe anti-aircraft missiles. A Territorial Army unit, 131 Commando Squadron, Royal Engineers, would also serve as part of the Brigade in time of war.

The Brigade's main role in NATO is the defence of northern Norway and all its members are trained skiers, spending three months every winter in Norway alongside 'Whiskey' Company, Royal Netherlands Marine Corps, and the Norwegian army practising arctic warfare. How-

LEFT A member of an SBS beach reconnaissance team stealthily measures the approach route for a raiding party.

ever, it has the flexibility to respond to a threat anywhere in the world and was embarked to the Falklands in record time aboard the liner *SS Canberra*, the Royal Fleet Auxiliary *Stromness* and the carrier *HMS Hermes*. They landed at San Carlos on 21 May; 40 Commando remained in reserve to secure the beachhead against a possible disaster while 42 and 45 Commandos headed for Port Stanley. The loss of the MV Atlantic Conveyor with its cargo of Chinook heli-

Canoeing and scuba diving are essential SBS skills.

copters meant it was only possible to airlift 42 Commando, so 45 Commando had to march (or 'yomp') in company with 3 Para across the whole width of the island to Port Stanley. The going was punishingly hard, the coarse tussocks of grass and soft mud combining with the weight of the men's bergens, weapons and ammunition to produce a number of sprained ankles. One sergeant commented colourfully that the advance looked 'more like the bloody retreat

M16 Armalite at the ready, and unusually wearing a 'dry' instead of a 'wet' suit, a member of the SBS wades ashore with a waterproof bag of kit.

using their Milan anti-tank launchers as 'bunker busters' and, although there were inevitable casualties, both attacks were a complete success and, as we have already seen, the Argentine commander surrendered on the afternoon of the 14th.

The other Royal Marine units active in the Falklands were the Mountain & Arctic Warfare Cadre and the Special Boat Squadron. The M&AW Cadre was originally formed as an instructional unit to train other Marines in mountain leadership, but in 1981 it was given an operational role as a deep arctic and mountain penetration unit for behind the lines reconnaissance and sabotage missions. Its members are all fully qualified Commandos who have already been selected as junior NCOs, so all volunteers for the Cadre are fit, tough and highly skilled from the start. Even so, the seven-day selection course is so arduous that on average less than half of the 'hopefuls' make it. The survivors spend another two weeks learning basic mountaineering skills in Wales, two weeks in Plymouth practising seaborne assaults using small raiding craft at night, then deploy to Norway where Norwegian army instructors teach them how to ski. After a period of Christmas leave they return to Norway for three months' intensive training in arctic survival, a course which culminates as in the SAS with a 40-mile hike carrying full kit across the rugged snow-covered terrain.

Even that is not the end of things for the M&AW Cadre recruits for they next spend several weeks practising navigation and pathfinding in Scotland, learning to parachute at Brize Norton, and being taught sniping techniques at Lympstone in Devon. Any member of the Cadre can kill a man at a range of over half a mile with a single shot. More time is spent practising advanced mountaineering techniques in Switzerland and the qualified recruits finally proceed to the Lake District to learn how themselves to be instructors. Graduation is celebrated by an annual month-long exercise code-

from Moscow'! But the Marines made it and by the end of the first week in June the Argentine forces in Port Stanley were surrounded.

Then, while 3 Para launched its assault on Mount Longdon during the night of 13/14 June, 42 Commando attacked Mount Harriet and 45 Commando Two Sisters. The men had been led to believe that the Argentines were all conscripts of low fighting standard and were disconcerted at the strength of the resistance, particularly from well-entrenched heavy machine gun positions. Several men were also mutilated by anti-personnel mines. The Marines retaliated by

Trying out a Jet Raider high speed, shallow draught assault boat.

named 'Ice Flip' in Switzerland. It can be appreciated that members of the Cadre are regarded with the highest respect by the toughest Commando! In the Falklands the Cadre was deployed ahead of the Task Force, alongside the SAS and SBS, reconnoitring enemy strengths and dispositions, and had one short, sharp but successful engagement with Argentine Commandos at Top Malo House, a skirmish which was conducted in such a classical manner that the Cadre later recreated it in a video film which is used for instructional purposes throughout the British armed forces.

Training for membership of the Special Boat Squadron is equally demanding and lasts a full year, but the emphasis is on different skills since the Squadron's primary role is reconnaissance of suitable landing sites for a larger amphibious task force, and this was their main task in the Falklands. As well as basic parachuting they learn the same HALO and HAHO techniques as the SAS and spend many weeks perfecting their canoeing and underwater swimming capabilities. They also learn how to exit from submerged submarines – the SBS team which landed on South Georgia in 1982 was actually flown to the South Atlantic in a Hercules from which they parachuted to a waiting sub and then made the journey ashore in Gemini inflatable boats. Otherwise, training is much the same as in the SAS or M&AW Cadre and the SBS is thus another elite within an elite. The same is true of Comacchio Group, based in Scotland with the principal task of defending Britain's offshore oil and gas rigs against terrorist attack. Scuba diving, parachuting and a high level of marksmanship are obviously demanded of members of this special force as well.

UNITED STATES OF AMERICA

The SEALs

The US Navy's SEAL (Sea-Air-Land) teams are the equivalent of the Special Boat Squadron and SAS Boat Troops, with whom they often interchange to swap information and techniques. They are generally regarded as the most highly skilled and trained fighting men in the American armed forces – though members of the other elite units might quibble with this judgement. Their origins go back to the wartime Underwater Demolition Teams (UDTs) formed in 1943 to assist in the difficult and dangerous task of clearing safe lanes through the German beach defences for the hundreds of landing craft used in the invasion of Normandy. Other UDT teams saw action at Guam, Iwo Jima and Okinawa. Similarly, during the Korean War they prepared

A UDT trainee rolls overboard from an inflatable boat which he will later have to clamber back aboard while it is being towed at high speed.

the way for the amphibious landing at Inchon. UDT personnel are all volunteers from the Navy and Marine Corps and are trained in every aspect of small boat usage as well as underwater swimming and, obviously, learning bomb disposal techniques and the use of a wide variety of explosives.

In 1960 a US Navy study suggested the need for even more specialized units to conduct deep penetration reconnaissance, sabotage and counter-terrorist operations from the sea or rivers, and in 1962 President John F Kennedy gave permission for the establishment of two new teams which were given the appropriate acronym SEALs. Recruited principally from the UDTs, they performed brilliantly during the Vietnam War from 1966 onwards, particularly in the Mekong Delta where they used the numerous rivers to gain access to their targets, sometimes

operating alongside South Vietnamese special forces, the 'Lin Dei Nugei Nghai'. Their missions included reconnaissance, identifying and destroying arms caches and jungle weapons' factories, laying ambushes in 'search and destroy' missions, capturing Vietcong officers for the intelligence information they could provide and even rescuing American servicemen from North Vietnamese prisoner-of-war compounds.

Subsequently the number of SEAL teams has been steadily increased and there are currently six with their Pacific headquarters at Coronado naval base, San Diego, California, and Atlantic headquarters at Norfolk, Virginia. Of these, No 6 is the specialist counter-terrorist unit and is solely comprised of proven veterans rather than recent recruits; it works closely with Delta (see page 62) and the British Comacchio Group.

SEALs during an infiltration/exfiltration exercise with a luridly camouflaged Bell UH-1 Huey helicopter.

SEAL detachments are normally also present at Subic Bay in the Philippines, as well as in Italy, Scotland and Puerto Rico. Each full team consists of 27 officers and 156 enlisted men divided into five platoons. Like the members of the SAS and SBS, they are 'go anywhere' soldiers who can operate equally well in temperate, jungle, desert or arctic conditions with only marginal preparations.

SEALs are recruited from volunteers who have already gone through the arduous 24-week UDT course held at Coronado. The first six weeks is a physical toughening-up process with long endurance marches and swims in the ocean. Recruits have to run everywhere and have to endure press-ups and other physical punishments at the drop of a hat. Less than half of each intake, perhaps 40 to 50 men, succeed in completing this initial 'tadpole' course. This

M16 Armalite and variants

The M16 family of firearms is, alongside the Soviet AK-47 quantitatively the most important in the postwar world and is used by the elite forces of most Western nations in one form or another in preference to their own army's standard rifle. Designed by Eugene Stoner for Armalite, the M16 assault rifle is actually manufactured by Colt and was adopted by the American army in 1961. Modifications introduced in 1966 after experience in Vietnam led to the designation M16A1 which is the most widely used variant. This gas-operated rifle fires 5.56 mm rounds from 20- or 30-round box magazines, either single-shot or fully automatic with a rate of fire of up to 150–200 rounds per minute.

However, it was found that firing in the automatic mode resulted in gross waste of ammunition so in 1981 a selector switch was introduced to give a three-round burst capability which is much more economical. Other changes in the M16A2 include a heavier barrel rebored to take the more powerful NATO standard SS109 5.56 mm cartridge which increases the weapon's range from 340 to 550 yards (310 to 500 m). All M16s can be fitted with the M203 40 mm grenade launcher beneath the barrel. This has a separate trigger and can fire a variety of fragmentation or smoke grenades. The M16 can also be fitted with a telescopic sight or a passive light intensifier.

A variant specifically developed for use by US special forces is the M15 Colt Commando. This has a shorter barrel with a prominent flash suppressor and a retractable butt, and is handier to use in the jungle or confined spaces such as buildings during fights against urban guerrillas, but effective range is only just over 200 yards (180 m). As a footnote, since it is often misunderstood, a flash suppressor at the end of a barrel is not designed to conceal the weapon from the enemy, but to help the man firing it from being temporarily blinded.

M16 with M203 grenade launcher.

course also includes a week-long escape and evasion exercise as well as advanced weapons training. The third part of the course involves learning basic hydrography for beach surveys, plus demolition and communications. Recruits then go to Fort Bonning for the army's three-week parachute course which is similar to the British one with the exception of balloons.

At this point the paths of those who are going to stay in the UDTs and those who are going into the SEALs partially diverge although they may overlap at later points, the former going on to an intensive 33-week course in the finer points of EOD which includes dealing with chemical, biological and even nuclear weapons. SEALs instead go on a 10-week course in the use of the Navy's Swimmer Delivery Vehicles (SDVs), which they will have learned something about already. These are small open craft propelled by an electric motor, the modern equivalent of the wartime 'human torpedos'. Being made mainly of non-ferrous materials, they are virtually undetectable to radar or sonar. These submersibles carry up to six men and have independent air supplies into which the men can plug to save the air in their backpack cylinders. The men also have to learn how to exit from and return to submerged sub-marines. The US Navy at the time of writing has three boats specifically converted for clandestine operations. Those SEALs who display the most proficiency in these techniques will be assigned to one of the Navy's two SDV teams whose job is to get the other six teams to their objectives.

As in the SAS and other truly elite forces, training never really stops and members of SEAL teams have to master HALO and HAHO techniques with steerable parachutes, study foreign languages and jungle warfare, learn counterterrorist tactics, signalling, advanced first aid and a variety of other skills including the most sophisticated unarmed combat techniques and the use of the Smith & Wesson Mk 22 silenced pistol. This is made of stainless steel so

phase culminates in 'Hell Week', a seven-day exercise always held under the wettest and coldest conditions possible with the recruits having to carry their inflatable boats everywhere in forced cross-country marches and then paddle them to a beach for a night infiltration exercise. This reduces the 'hopefuls' by about half again.

For the survivors, the next few weeks involve even longer open sea swims and instruction in small boat handling and scuba diving at a variety of depths using different breathing mixtures. Classroom work is principally concerned with explosive ordnance disposal (EOD) but also involves tactics and survival, and this part of the

Members of the Green Berets during a gruelling joint training exercise with US Navy SEALs.

Two scenes from life in the UDTs and SEALs. **LEFT** Recruits unable to keep up during a 4 mile (6 km) run are punished by press-ups on the beach. **ABOVE** The pressure is on again as they deploy an inflatable boat during a readiness inspection.

it will not suffer in seawater and was introduced during the Vietnam War to deal with guard dogs. With somewhat sick humour, it is generally called the 'hush puppy'. Naturally, they also train with other NATO and Warsaw Pact weapons and regularly use shotguns in 'close' combat situations. SEALs are also the only soldiers known to have regularly used the Stoner/Cadillac-Gage model 63 assault rifle in Vietnam. This imaginative weapons system used interchangeable parts to allow it to impersonate anything from a sub-machine gun to a heavy machine gun with tripod sustained-fire mount proved to be a 'jack of all trades and master of none' and was soon dropped.

Although it sounds even more like science fiction, selected members of the SEALs also learn to operate alongside dolphins. The dolphin is not normally an aggressive mammal, although a shark does not stand a chance against one and there have been several instances of dolphins coming to the rescue of humans in trouble

in the sea. About 60 dolphins reliably reported to have been trained to kill on command were used during the Vietnam War but whether they received a Unit Citation is not publicly recorded! In the SEALs (and their dolphins), the US Navy has one of the finest bodies of special forces in the world, and they further proved their worth in 1983 when a team was first ashore on the Caribbean island of Grenada to help in the rescue of imprisoned American medical students, even though the main part of the operation was carried out by the Marines, Rangers and 82nd Airborne Division.

US Marine Corps

The US Marine Corps is the world's largest elite force with a current establishment of nearly 200,000 men and women. During the Vietnam War they took part in almost all the major operations using helicopters or landing craft to reach

ABOVE Pump-action shotguns are favoured close-quarter weapons among many elite forces, including the SEALs. **OPPOSITE** US Marines – seen here after being dropped by a Boeing Vertol CH-47 helicopter – have to learn to live and fight under all climatic extremes.

their targets and have subsequently been deployed in Grenada, Beirut and Panama to name but three recent examples. They suffered over 100,000 dead, wounded or missing in Vietnam and 241 killed by a single terrorist bomb attack in Beirut in October 1983, which demonstrates something of the carnage of what has been called 'war in peace'.

Today there are four Marine Divisions and four complementary Air Wings. A division consists of three infantry regiments, each of three battalions, plus an artillery regiment, a tank battalion, an armoured amphibian battalion with LVTP-7 Amtracks, a light armoured assault battalion with M2/M3 Bradley mechanized combat vehicles and various other supporting services. The infantry battalions are smaller today than in the past but still consist of the traditional three rifle companies, one headquarters company and a support company. The total strength of

ABOVE Marine riflemen during an assault demonstration. **LEFT** In a scene enacted many times over the last 50 years, Marines wade ashore from a landing craft.

each division averages 17–18,000 men.

Basic training at one of the two 'boot' camps at San Diego or Parris Island lasts 11 weeks, officer candidates then going on to Quantico. This is designed to instil physical toughness and confidence as well as smartness, discipline and marksmanship. Those who pass go on to learn more specialist skills according to aptitude, learning how to board and exit landing craft and helicopters. The Marine Corps needs specialist signallers, drivers, combat engineers, medics and men in a dozen and more skilled trades but only the top of each intake can volunteer for the Marines' own elite, the Reconnaissance Units or 'Recons'.

The idea for the Recons was devised by Lieutenant-General Bernard Trainor who served as an exchange officer with the British Royal Marines in 1958–59 and was impressed by the Commando operations in Cyprus. On his return to the United States he pressed for the creation within the USMC of small commando-style units to operate behind enemy lines on reconnaissance missions during which they would, if necessary, remain hidden in one spot for days at a time observing enemy troop movements and reporting back by radio. The first teams were established by 1961 and saw extensive service in Vietnam, usually operating in seven-man squads on 'Sting Ray' missions, plotting Vietcong positions and either calling in artillery or air strikes or taking them out in ambushes. Later, the strength of the squads was reduced to four men as in the SAS or SBS.

Training for the Recon teams is very similar to that of the SBS and includes swimming, scuba diving, canoeing, parachuting, forward artillery observation, beach reconnaissance and demolition work. Today, each Marine division has a Recon battalion of about 500 men. Competition to get into the Recons is keen but as in the British armed forces, only the very best pass the arduous course to win the green and gold winged parachute badge with the legend 'USMC RECON'.

Finally, the four Marine Air Wings consist of between 18 and 21 squadrons with 286–315 fixed-wing aircraft and helicopters. These include F-4 Phantom and F-18 Hornet fighter/ attack aircraft, A-4 Skyhawk, A-6 Intruder and AV-8A/B Harrier attack aircraft, KC-130 in-flight refuelling tankers and a mixture of AH-1, CH-35 and -46 and UH-1 utility, reconnaissance and attack helicopters.

The Rangers

The US Army's wartime Ranger battalions formed by Orlando Darby were disbanded after the Korean War although a cadre remained at Fort Benning as a leadership school to train the army in light infantry tactics. They were not activated during the Vietnam War but in 1975 it was decided to create two new battalions. These were placed on standby alert during the Tehran Embassy crisis in 1980 but were stood down after the failure of the operation 'Eagle Claw' rescue mission (see page 63) and did not see action until they were sent in to Grenada in 1983 where they put up a creditable performance against the Cuban troops on the island.

In 1984 a third battalion was raised and the current status of the 75th Ranger Regiment, to give it its full title, is a regimental headquarters

of some 130 men and three light infantry battalions of about 575. Volunteers for the Rangers will normally have gone through the Ranger School before applying, and have to be parachute-trained before they can be accepted. The school is a unique institution because of its survival when there were no active Ranger battalions. The course there lasts 58 days and teaches volunteers the skills of navigation, survival, advanced weapons handling, close combat with knives or bare hands, and mountaineering.

Those who have passed this course, and completed at least eight parachute jumps, have to go through a three-week selection course called the Ranger Indoctrination Program. This stresses physical prowess but embraces all aspects of fieldcraft and weapons' handling as

OPPOSITE Marines storm ashore from LVTP-7 Amtrack amphibious armoured personnel carriers while Sikorsky S-58 helicopters hover overhead. **BELOW** On the beachhead, a battery of M102 105 mm howitzers goes into action.

well as the technique of abseiling from helicopters into jungle or mountain terrain. The intake for each Program is small, between 10 and 30 men, so it is possible to give instruction almost on an individual basis which results in a very high pass rate of 70 per cent on average. Those who pass are entitled to wear the Ranger flash and black beret and serve a normal tour of 24 months including four two-week leave periods, although the tour can be increased by up to six months under special circumstances. Rangers have to be young, fit and 'on the bounce', and rarely stay in the line over the age of 22 although many members who wish to re-enlist find a welcome reception in one of the other army corps and, as with the SAS, this helps in spreading knowledge and skills around.

The 75th Ranger Regiment is one of the select units which fall under US Special Operations Command. This has gradually evolved since

the need for centralized control of special forces was realized at the beginning of the 1980s and is a rather strange organization which since 1987 has overseen the SEALs, the Rangers and the Special Operations Forces Groups – popularly known as the 'Green Berets' – but not the USMC or airborne and airmobile divisions. These instead form components in the Rapid Deployment Force. US Special Operations .Command (USSOC) liaises directly with the Central and Defense Intelligence Agencies and National Security Agency (CIA, DIA and NSA), with their own close links to Britain's MI5 and 6, GCHQ and the SAS. The organization includes a psychological warfare and a civilian affairs corps. It is, you might say, a global trouble-shooter.

Face blackened with camouflage cream, a US soldier holds his sub-machine-gun at the ready.

Special Operations Forces – the 'Green Berets'

The role of the US Special Operations Forces is nowhere better expressed than in the words of their founding officer. Colonel Aaron Bank was a wartime veteran of the Office of Strategic Services (OSS) with extensive experience of clandestine operations behind Japanese lines in Burma. Against opposition from both the army and the newly-formed CIA, both of which thought they knew better, Bank formed a new school at Fort Bragg in North Carolina to train volunteers 'to infiltrate by land, sea or air, deep into enemy-occupied territory and organize the resistance/guerrilla potential to conduct special forces' operations with emphasis on guerrilla warfare'.

At this point, with the Cold War at its chilliest and heavy fighting continuing in Korea, Bank was one of the few who saw very early that the postwar world was going to see a revolution in unconventional warfare conducted by nationalistic or politically motivated forces who would disappear into the civilian background. The assistance of the local population in identifying them and helping to fight them would be extremely important.

Bank had very clear ideas about the sort of men he needed in his new force, whose first component was the 10th Special Forces (SF) Group (Airborne). He wanted trained veterans with airborne, Ranger or wartime special forces' experience who had proved themselves reliable and willing to learn new tricks. Because of their envisaged behind-the-lines role, he also wanted linguists and got a good response from European and Asiatic expatriates who knew they could acquire American citizenship by enlisting in the armed forces. In this respect the SF became something of an equivalent to the French Foreign Legion and still retains something of a multinational flavour. This is reinforced by mixed training exercises with the special forces of other nations.

How the sobriquet 'Green Berets' was arrived at is a story in itself. General Bank was a staunch admirer of the British Commandos and thought that nothing could be more appropriate than for his new force to wear a similar piece of headgear. This presumption of 'elitism' brought howls of rage from many senior army officers and its wearing was discontinued until 1961 when President Kennedy visited Fort Bragg and ordered its reinstatement! In mutual respect, after the President's assassination the Green Berets renamed their training school the John F Kennedy Special Warfare Center.

By this time there were three SF Groups, the 1st, 7th and 10th, and as American involvement grew in Vietnam there was further expansion until by 1964 there were seven, the newcomers being the 3rd, 5th, 6th and 8th. Each was given a specific geographical region as its particular concern. The 1st and 5th drew South-East Asia, including the Philippines and Taiwan, the 3rd Africa, the 6th the Middle East and the 8th Central and South America; the 7th saw varied duty in Germany, Vietnam and Central America while the 10th was divided between the continental United States and Germany. The 3rd saw service in support of government forces in the Congo, Ethiopia, Guinea and Kenya and the 6th in Iran, Jordan, Saudi Arabia, Turkey and Pakistan, largely acting as advisors to train indiginent troops in counter-insurgency tactics, but it was of course in Vietnam that the Green Berets came into the limelight. (They have more recently, of course, been involved in Colombia and Panama.)

The first men of the 1st Special Forces Group arrived as advisors in South Vietnam in 1957, shortly after the French withdrawal and the country's partitioning. Over the next five years the political situation gradually worsened and by 1962 there were some 4,000 American servicemen and women in Vietnam. At this point the Green Berets got involved in what was known as the Civil Irregular Defense Group programme designed to train the montagnards from the highlands in which the borders of Laos, Cambodia (Kampuchea) and South Vietnam met. These tribesmen do not class themselves as Vietnamese and were willing subjects for the Green Berets' 'hearts and minds' campaign, readily establishing fortified centres and eagerly adapting to modern smallarms despite an almost total lack of education. By 1964 some 18,000 of them were acting in a local defence and reconnaissance role for the US and South Vietnamese armies, operating out of fortified villages whose defences were progressively strengthened as the conflict escalated.

In this ame year the Green Berets introduced a new type of unit, the Studies and Observation Groups, a polite and innocuous name for units whose task was infiltrating the territory of surrounding countries on what were essentially espionage missions to pinpoint hostile troop build-ups. The 'SOGs' included SEALs and USMC Recon personnel as well as Green Berets. This development, coupled with Vietcong attacks on the mnontagnard villages, led in 1965 to the creation of Mobile Strike Force teams to attack Vietcong training camps over the borders. In both forms of mission, as well as in training 'loyal' Vietnamese, Laotian and Cambodian troops, the Green Berets acored a high success rate. They also undertook many reconnaissance, sabotage and ambush sorties as well as rescue missions – Son Tay on 21 November 1970 being the most publicized such attempt even though it was unsuccessful because of PoWs had been moved. When the last US Special Forces were finally withdrawn from Vietnam in 1971 they had earned 11,790 medals including 17 Medals of Honor, the US equivalent of the Victoria Cross.

From 1969 onwards there was a gradual rundown of Green Beret units. In that year the 3rd Group was deactivated, followed by the 6th in 1971, the 8th in 1972 and the 1st in 1974. With subsequent changes there are today four active

and four reserve SF units. The active ones are the reconstituted 1st based at Fort Lewis, Washington; the 5th at Fort Bragg; the 7th at Fort Benning and the 10th at Fort Devens, Massachusetts. One battalion from the 1st Group is stationed on Okinawa, one from the 5th at Fort Campbell, Kentucky, one from the 7th in Panama and one from the 10th at Bad Tölz, Germany. The reserve Groups are the 11th at Fort Meade, Maryland, the 12th at Arlington Heights, Illinois, the 19th (National Guard) at Salt Lake City, Utah, and the 20th (National Guard) at Birmingham, Alabama. All fall under the control of the US 1st Special Operations Command.

Each Group comprises three battalions which contains a headquarters company known as the 'C' Team and three companies known as 'B' Teams. Each 'B' Team is made up of five or six 'A' Teams, the Green Berets' normal tactical unit. These are larger than their equivalents in the SAS, being composed of 10 men plus a Lieutenant or Warrant Officer as executive officer and a Captain as CO. All the men are NCOs and each has his own speciality. There is an operations and an assistant operations sergeant, a heavy weapons and a light weapons leader, two medics, two radio operators and one engineer. As each member of the Green Berets has already had airborne or Ranger training, a description will not be repeated. Specialist training for the above roles lasts between 16 and 25 weeks although it is longer for medics – 43 weks including a month working in the casualty department of a hospital. Many SF personnel voluntarily take extra training in such skills as scuba diving, mountaineering, jungle warfare tactics, intelligence analysis and interpretation, demolition and escape and evasion. In fact, as in all special forces, training never really stops.